The FIRST BOOK of SALT

The FIRST BOOK of
SALT

by Olive Burt

Illustrated with photographs

FRANKLIN WATTS, INC.
575 Lexington Ave., N.Y. 10022

For Park —
who first drew my attention to the value of salt

Library of Congress Catalog Card Number: 65-11744
© Copyright 1965 by Franklin Watts, Inc.
Printed in the United States of America
by Polygraphic Company of America
1 2 3 4 5

CONTENTS

THE MINERAL WITH MANY USES   1

WE MUST HAVE SALT   3

ANIMALS, TOO, NEED SALT   5

SOME PLANTS LIKE SALT   10

MAN AND SALT   12

WHAT IS SALT?   14

WHERE DOES SALT COME FROM?   14

SALT IN THE AIR   16

OLD DAYS — OLD WAYS   16

SALT, THE POWERFUL   22

SALT IN GOVERNMENT AND SOCIAL LIFE   24

SALT BUILDS ROADS   26

SALT AND CITIES   27

SALT IN COLONIAL AMERICA   30

SALT IN THE AMERICAN REVOLUTION   32

SALT IN THE WEST   33

OTHER SALT FINDS   35

SALT IN THE CIVIL WAR   36

NEW DAYS, NEW WAYS   39

SOLAR EVAPORATION TODAY   46

MINING SALT   48

PLENTY OF SALT   55

LOST LAKES   57

SALT IN INDUSTRY AND DAILY LIFE   60

DO YOU KNOW —   60

WORDS SALTMAKERS USE   62

INDEX   63

The world's debt to salt is pictured in this beautiful mosaic mural. From left to right, it shows salt's use as payment for soldiers; as food; to preserve fish; and for baking. On the far right is a worker at a salt mine (Morton Salt Company)

THE MINERAL WITH MANY USES

SALT HAS BEEN CALLED "the mineral with fourteen thousand uses." Many of the things we handle every day owe something to this wonderful material.

Not only does our food taste better when it is salted at the table, but even before it arrives there it may have been treated with salt, either to preserve it or to add to its flavor.

Most canned foods need salt. Today salt can be bought in small tablets made especially for the various kinds of food and the different sizes of cans. As the cans pass along a conveyor belt at the factory, the tablets are dropped into them. Thus, exactly the right amount of salt is placed in each can.

Baking soda is obtained from salt.

Salt can be made into many useful chemicals. Salt or chemicals taken from salt have a part in preserving animal hides and making shoe leather. Fabrics are either bleached or colored with the aid of salt products. And salt products are used in the manufacture of man-made fabrics such as nylon and orlon.

Glass is nearly one-sixth soda ash, taken from salt. Soaps and plastics are made with the aid of salt products.

Salt is thrown by the shovelful over hides, to preserve them (Morton Salt Company)

Salt products play an important part in the making of automobiles. They help produce the hard lacquer finish, the stainless steel trim, the strong steel of working parts, perhaps even the tires.

Because pure salt crystals made in certain ways are completely transparent they are used in the making of lenses for precision optical instruments.

Salt is valuable as an antiseptic and as a relief for aching feet and muscles. People have long known how beneficial saltwater baths are, and many a health resort has prospered near salt springs. Salt can even be rubbed on the teeth as a cleanser, instead of toothpaste.

Sodium, one of the ingredients of salt, is the best-known heat conductor. It is used in airplane, truck, and bus engines, and in nuclear reactors. As the engine heats up, the sodium melts and sloshes around. It strikes the hottest parts of the engine and carries the heat away to the valve stems, where it is cooled. Sodium is also used in making the additive for anti-knock gasoline.

In winter, salt is used to keep streets and highways free of ice and

In winter, salt is used to remove ice from the highway (International Salt Company)

snow. When combined with the snow and ice, it forms a mixture with a lower freezing point than that of water, and so has a melting effect.

These are only a few of the ways in which salt works for us — and new uses are being found all the time. Just recently, researchers at the University of Utah found that if glass is given a bath in molten salt it becomes much harder to break. But it can be bent, and is called bendable glass. It will have a use in automobiles, and will greatly lessen the danger from broken glass in accidents.

WE MUST HAVE SALT

"PLEASE PASS THE SALT."

How often we say this without ever thinking how important salt really is to us.

Salt, air, and water are the three natural substances that man has used ever since he first appeared upon the earth. All three are necessary to life.

Scientists tell us that in the warm, salty waters at the edges of the first seas, land life began. From the ocean, living creatures crept out upon the shore to begin a new and different kind of existence. They kept a part of the sea in their bodies, however. Even to this day the makeup of human blood has some elements in common with that of seawater.

Our bodies are formed of tiny cells which might be compared to minute building blocks. These cells are collected into various organs — the heart, lungs, kidneys, and so on. The cells are bathed in a circulating fluid, which supplies them with the elements they need for living. It is made up of blood cells carried in a salty fluid called plasma. If this fluid dried up or if the salt were removed from it, the body cells would die. Some doctors say that if every trace of salt were removed from our bodies, we would not live more than forty-eight hours.

The blood of other animals, like that of human beings, contains salt. Those groups of people who eat a great deal of raw meat and fish do not

3

have to add salt to their food. They get the necessary amounts from the blood of the animals they consume. That is why some Eskimos and some African tribes do not use salt as other people do.

Cooked foods lose a large part of their natural salt. Where people eat cooked meat, or green plants, they find it wise to add salt to their food.

The amount of salt in our bodies is naturally regulated so that it will be right for our size. And it must be renewed daily, as we are constantly losing salt through perspiration, tears, and urine.

Most of us eat more salt than we really need, because we have grown to like it. The salt we take into our stomachs is absorbed into the blood. The body keeps just as much as it needs and gets rid of the rest through the kidneys or pores. If, for some reason, the necessary amount of salt is not being supplied in our food, the body hangs on to what it has and stops giving off salt. It does this without our even thinking about it.

When the body cannot get the salt it needs, there is trouble. Salt hunger is terrible. Animals have been known to eat wood or rags or leather in an attempt to get salt. One farmer wanted to sue the government because his cow died from eating the paint on an airfield signal, but he was told that it was his own fault. If he had given the cow the salt she needed, she would not have eaten the paint.

Experiments with rabbits show that when they do not have salt they become paralyzed and finally die. Experiments with people cannot be carried that far, of course, but when human beings do not get enough salt or when they lose too much through heavy perspiration, they show signs of distress. Nowadays when people work in the tropics or other hot places they are given salt tablets, which look something like aspirin tablets and generally contain five or ten grains of salt. These tablets are very helpful in restoring the body's salt balance.

When Napoleon's soldiers were retreating from Moscow in the winter of 1812 they perished by the thousands, partly because they could not get enough salt. As a result of this lack they could not bear fatigue, their wounds would not heal, and their food could not be properly digested.

4

This pet raccoon bur-rows into his master's pocket for a piece of salt

Necessary as salt is, though, in some cases a person's body cannot handle it properly. In such cases a doctor may put the person on a "salt-free diet," and tell him to eat little or no salt, though of course he still gets some in his food. Such a diet must be followed only under a doctor's care, as it is not safe for a person to decide on it for himself.

ANIMALS, TOO, NEED SALT

ANIMALS SUCH AS lions and tigers, which eat raw meat, do not have to find extra salt. But those animals that live on plants must get extra salt somewhere. In the jungle there may be a rock outcropping or a salt spring which makes a lick where all kinds of animals come together to get this needed mineral.

Placed on a short pole, pressed blocks of salt are out of the dirt and within easy reach of the animals (U. S. Department of Agriculture)

In the United States many such licks are known. Here, in earlier days, great herds of buffalo and deer came to lick salt. And before the buffalo there were the huge mastodons that once roamed the country. When a settlement grew up around such a lick, the name of the town may still show it, as with French Lick, Indiana, and Big Bone Lick, Kentucky. The huge ribs of the mammoths found there gave the latter place its name.

Nowadays cows and horses and other farm animals are not left free to wander about and find salt licks. Their owners must supply the extra salt they need. The simplest way is to throw lumps of rock salt on the ground, where the animals can find it.

Usually, however, modern stock-owners buy five-pound "salt licks" or fifty-pound "salt blocks," especially made. The large blocks generally have a hole in the center so that they can be placed on a short pole, out of the dirt and in easy reach of the animals.

These salt blocks are manufactured scientifically. Experts carefully test the soil of the area where the blocks are sold, to find out if any needed

Crystals of granulated salt are thoroughly blended with added minerals in the factory's screw mixing machine (International Salt Company)

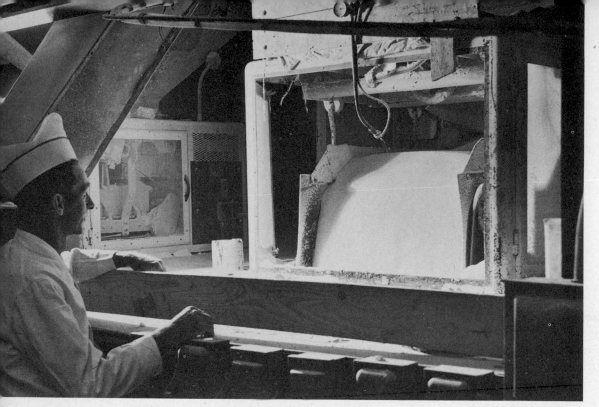

Iodine is added to table salt as it passes on a continuous conveyor belt under a spray solution of potassium iodide (International Salt Company)

mineral element is lacking in it. Animals must provide their bodies with a number of minerals besides salt. If any of these minerals do not exist in the soil, they will not be found in the hay and grass and grain that grow there. Accordingly, if the experts find that something is lacking, they simply add it to the salt block.

The most common element added is iodine, which helps to prevent goiter. Iodine is often added to table salt for the same purpose. The iodine does not change the color of the salt. If iron is added to a block, it makes a dull-red color. Sulphur makes a yellow block, cobalt a blue one. Adding minerals to salt blocks has done a great deal to improve the stock on American farms.

Our pets, too, require extra salt, for many of them have no way of

Millions of migratory birds stop each year at the Bird Refuge in Utah, where they find the salty marshlands and the food they are used to (Peter J. Van Huizen, U. S. Fish and Wildlife Service)

finding it, because they are kept rather close to home. For these small animals the salt companies sell "pet licks," which may be found in pet stores. The animals are grateful for the salt and show finer coats and better dispositions because of it.

Many wildfowl are used to salty marshlands, yet when they fly south in the winter or north in the spring they often have to travel great distances without finding a stopping place like the one where they usually live. In many places, marshy land areas have been set aside as bird refuges where these traveling fowl may rest on their long journeys. On a northern arm of the Great Salt Lake in Utah, 64,000 acres have been diked off to make a safe refuge for bird travelers.

This salt hay harvested on the shores of Antelope Island in Utah's Great Salt Lake is fed to cattle and buffalo, who thrive on it (Ray G. Jones)

SOME PLANTS LIKE SALT

MOST PLANTS DO NOT thrive well on a salty diet, but some, such as certain kinds of grasses and reeds, and mangrove trees, have become fitted to live in the salty water that feeds their roots. Some such grasses are good fodder, and animals like them. A small herd of buffalo and a large herd of cows on Antelope Island in the Great Salt Lake show fine, sleek coats. Their owners say that this sleekness is due to the hay gathered along the shore of the island.

It is claimed that strawberries grown in a salty soil are larger and sweeter than others. Even cut flowers keep longer if a pinch of salt is added to the water in which their stems are placed.

But too much salt is harmful for plants. Nothing at all grows on the salt flats of Utah and Nevada. The scanty vegetation of many deserts is due to the salt in the soil as well as to the lack of water.

Many deserts, like this one in Texas, owe their scanty vegetation to the salty soil as well as to the lack of water (Texas Highway Department)

Huge salt crystals form on the edge of the Great Salt Lake in cold, calm weather, when fresh water flows in and fails to mix with the heavier brine (Utah State Historical Society)

MAN AND SALT

IN THE DAYS when primitive man ate raw meat he probably did not feel the need to add salt to his diet. As he became civilized and began to eat more vegetables and to cook his food, however, he found that his body demanded extra salt.

At first he may have done as the animals did — he may have found a place where he could lick salt, perhaps at the edge of a lake or spring. Soon he must have realized that he could pick up lumps of the tasty stuff and carry it away with him, to use as he wanted. Still later — for changes of this kind came very slowly — he learned that he could trade some of his extra chunks for something else he wanted. The first salt trade had begun.

No one knows how many years went by before man learned to add salt to his food. But he did learn. Objects found in Belgian caves show that men were putting salt into cooked foods five thousand years ago. And at some early time man discovered that salt would preserve food from spoiling.

We know that three thousand years ago the Trojans were using salt to preserve fish. And we know that the early Egyptians used salt not only to preserve food, but also to embalm the dead bodies of their most famous people.

For a long time, man must have been content to use salt only as he found it. But slowly into his awakening brain the idea must have drifted that he himself could do something to add to his supply of this needed substance.

He must have observed that seawater, washed into shallow pools, disappeared after a while and that salt was left. Why, then, couldn't a man dig a ditch to let the sea run into a neighboring hollow at high tide? There, when the tide had lowered, water would remain. It would evaporate, and soon there would be salt. He tried this and it worked.

At some early time, too, man had learned that fire could "drive away" — or evaporate — water. Perhaps if he boiled seawater he could drive away the liquid and get the salt it held. Maybe man did not reason this out. Maybe he discovered entirely by accident how to boil seawater for salt: a pot left too long over the fire may have showed a crust of salt at its bottom. But whether he worked it out in his mind or discovered it by chance, early man learned to make salt by boiling seawater.

For convenience's sake we speak of "making" or "manufacturing" salt. Actually, man does not make salt. All he does is take it out of the water or the ground where he finds it. He may refine it, purify it, add to it, but he does not manufacture it.

WHAT IS SALT?

JUST WHAT IS this substance, salt?

The word "salt" is used for many different chemicals, but in this book the term is employed only to mean what we all know as common salt, in any of its forms. Even this common salt is called different names by different people.

To a geologist — a person who studies rocks — salt is a rocky mineral called *halite*. To a chemist it is a compound, *sodium chloride*. To most of us it is a condiment — something added to food to make it more tasty.

Any natural substance found in the earth's crust — and which never has been alive — is called a mineral. Salt is a mineral made up of two elements, sodium and chlorine. (An element is a simple substance — one that cannot be further broken down into separate parts; it is "all of a piece," one might say.)

WHERE DOES SALT COME FROM?

THERE IS A salt ingredient in many of the rocks that make up the earth's crust. As rain strikes the rocks and wears them away it carries dissolved particles of salt into brooks and streams and rivers, and so, on down to the sea or to a lake. There the sun beats down and causes some of the water to evaporate. But the salt is left behind, and as time goes on it makes the remaining water saltier and saltier. Salt lake or ocean waters are an important source of our salt.

Before people knew the real reason for the saltiness of the ocean, they made up stories about it. Children in the Philippine Islands were told that in the Beginning the Great Giant was building a white palace of crystal salt bricks. As his workmen were carrying a load of these bricks across a bamboo bridge over an arm of the sea, the bridge broke. The bricks fell into the water and dissolved, making the whole sea salty.

14

*At Searles Lake, California, miles of salt surface, dry and hard, have been left by
the shrinking lake (American Potash & Chemical Corporation)*

In some north European countries, people believed that the salt in the
ocean came from tears shed by unhappy folk. And there is an old German
tale about a man with a magic salt mill. As he was grinding salt one day
he dropped his mill into the ocean. And there it lies to this day, grinding
away, constantly adding more salt to the sea.

SALT IN THE AIR

WE THINK OF RAIN and running water as fresh, or free of salt, but there is generally some salt in the freshest water.

Even the air carries some salt. If you have ever stood on a rocky headland by the sea, you have felt the salt spray sting your eyes and have tasted the salt on your lips. Wind picks up the salt in the spray and carries it inland. Finally, rain washes this so-called cyclic (sī-klik) salt out of the air and onto the ground. Once there, it gradually finds its way back through rivers to the sea.

Folks living near the Great Salt Lake in Utah are sometimes annoyed by cyclic salt. After a windstorm over the lake, rain spots windows and windshields with salt, which is hard to remove. Sometimes birds flying low over the lake get their wings so weighted with salt from the spray that they cannot fly. They drop to the ground or the surface of the lake, and die. When early-day trappers told of seeing great pelicans and seagulls wholly encrusted with salt, folks did not believe them. But today we know this often happens.

Cyclic salt sometimes falls unnoticed on the land. Every year, England with its miles of rocky coast receives from twenty-four to thirty-six pounds of salt an acre. British Guiana, on the north coast of South America, yearly gets one hundred pounds an acre. Most amazing of all is the distance this salt is carried in India. Sambhar Lake, in the northwestern part of that country, receives three thousand tons of salt a year, carried on hot, dry winds from the ocean, four hundred miles away.

OLD DAYS — OLD WAYS

SCHOLARS DISAGREE as to which method man first used in making salt — evaporating salt water or boiling it. Perhaps the two methods developed independently in different parts of the world. We do know that the Chinese were boiling brine for salt some five thousand years ago. But

16

Agricola, a scientist who wrote about salt almost five hundred years ago, said that evaporation in shallow pools was the first method used by man.

Producing salt by the use of the sun's rays is called the *solar evaporation* method. (Solar means "of the sun.") Through past ages a great deal of the world's salt was obtained by this method, though it had several drawbacks. It could be used only during a long, hot, dry spell, because a heavy rainfall would add fresh water to the evaporating salt water and so delay the saltmaking process. Agricola thought it was this problem that caused men to try boiling the water.

At first, in solar evaporating, natural hollow places near the sea were used for salt ponds. This was done in Italy, in the Cape Verde and Caribbean islands, and in other hot, dry regions. The remains of just such natural salt ponds may be seen today in Key West, Florida.

This old engraving shows an early works for taking salt from ocean water by solar evaporation. A. *Sea.* B. *Pool.* C. *Gate.* D. *Trenches.* E. *Salt basins.* F. *Rake.* G. *Shovel (New York Public Library)*

Later it was found that more and cleaner salt could be obtained if artificial ponds were built. These could be given a hard, impenetrable floor of clay or wood. Dirt, insects, and plants could be kept out more easily. Such artificial ponds were built in France, Spain, and Portugal. At one time, Portuguese salt was considered the best in the world.

People in other places tried other ways of getting cleaner salt. In some parts of France, stakes were driven into the ponds and the salt collecting on them was later scraped off. In other areas clean rocks were used for the salt to cling to.

In north European countries, where there were no long, hot summers, the boiling method was generally used. Of course, salt obtained in this way was freer of dirt and other unwanted substances than was that made by solar evaporation. In the early days the salt water was simply boiled in an iron pot over an open fire. Later, brick ovens were built, with large iron boilers set permanently over the fires. In early Chinese saltworks, bamboo pipes were used to bring the brine, the mixture of salt and water, from the salt wells. Water buffalo worked the treadmills that ran the pumps, and brick ovens and huge boilers were used.

A sixteenth-century engraving shows saltmakers boiling salt water over an open fire

A Chinese artist of 2700 B.C. *shows ash from salt plants being boiled in a kettle with seawater. The liquid was evaporated until an egg could be floated in it (Worcester Salt Company)*

Less advanced peoples obtained salt in various other ways. Some early German tribes set logs afire, then threw seawater over them. The water went off in steam, and salt was left on the logs.

When Caesar marched into England in 55 B.C. he brought along a number of saltmakers to teach the savages how to obtain salt by the Roman method of solar evaporation. He found, however, that the natives had their own way. They placed logs in kettles of boiling seawater, then scraped off the salt that clung to the logs after the water had boiled away. In parts of Thailand, even today, a similar method is used. Seawater is thrown over hot rocks, from which the salt is then scraped.

Where there were no salt deposits or salt springs, inventive folks found other ways to get salt. Seaweeds and salt plants could be burned, and salt could be washed out of the remaining ash. This method was used in the interior of Asia.

19

In the South Pacific Islands and among some California Indians the people simply dipped their food in seawater, or used seawater as a sauce for fruits and vegetables.

Quicker than either boiling or solar evaporating was simply gathering rock salt, especially when it was found aboveground. Then it needed only to be crushed. Such salt breaks into lumps uneven in size, and is often bitter to the taste because of impurities. When the rock salt is belowground it must be mined, like other underground minerals.

Mountains of rock salt in North Africa, around the Dead Sea, and in South America have been worked for thousands of years. It is said that for their religious rites Egyptian priests preferred the rock salt of the Sahara to sea salt.

The most famous salt mine in the world is at Wieliczka, near Krakow, Poland. Rock salt has been mined here for more than a thousand years. In early times the workmen sat in rope swings hung from the walls. They dug out the salt with hand picks, letting it fall into their canvas aprons. When each workman's apron was full of salt he climbed down and emptied it into a cart. Donkeys drew the loaded carts to the surface. Working by hand, the miners could carve out fantastic sculptured figures. In the eighty-mile-long mine they fashioned a whole glittering village, complete with church, marketplace, streets, houses, and a stream on which boats floated. The church held an altar and religious statues; the marketplace was filled with fruits and vegetables, all carved from salt.

American workers, using modern machinery, do not ordinarily spend time carving buildings and statues in the salt mines. This office, however, carved entirely of salt, is 1,137 feet belowground in a mine under the city of Detroit, Michigan (International Salt Company)

Some European and Asian salt mines were formerly notorious for their terrible working conditions (From an old engraving, New York Public Library)

This mine is now behind the Iron Curtain, and visitors from the western world cannot see it. But there is doubt that the workers in this famous mine still are allowed to act as sculptors. The latest pictures of the mine show modern machinery doing the work. And where modern, electrically powered machines work there is little opportunity for a man to show his creative skill.

Other parts of Europe have similar mines in which workmen have carved statues and frescoes. One at Bad Ischl near Salzburg, Austria, is open to visitors.

The United States has several great salt mines, but modern machinery is used in them and the men have no time for fanciful carving. In one mine under Detroit, Michigan, a small office building was carved from the salt and was used for a while. Now the mine has extended far from this point and the building is abandoned.

In the 1880's the salt mines of Russia became notorious throughout the world. Prisoners were condemned to spend the rest of their lives working in these mines, and many stories were told of the terrible conditions in them. From these reports came the saying, "Back to the salt mines," a phrase which American workers sometimes jokingly use at the end of a vacation or a coffee break, on their return to work.

21

SALT, THE POWERFUL

FOR THOUSANDS OF YEARS, salt exerted great power in the world. For one thing, it had a religious importance held by no other common substance. Since the sun "drew up" seawater, leaving salt for man, salt was considered a special gift from the sun god. Because it was necessary to life and could preserve foods from spoiling, it was thought to have sacred power.

For a long time, men did not try to find new and better ways of obtaining salt, because tampering with the ancient methods was considered sacrilegious and dangerous.

Salt was used in many ancient religious ceremonies, some of which have continued to this day. The Bible has thirty-two references to salt, chiefly in connection with sacrifices and covenants. The covenant of salt was said to be the most binding of all pledges. Ancient Greeks offered salt to the gods before each meal. The Hebrews made a salt offering to Jehovah at harvesttime. The goddess of salt was one of the four chief Aztec deities. Salt Woman is one of the holy people of the Navahos, and Salt Man is a Hopi war god.

Along with the belief in the sacredness of salt went the idea that the Devil hated and feared it. One medieval abbot scattered salt in his church so that the Devil would not bother the worshipers by making them cough or sneeze or go to sleep during the sermon.

Many superstitions grew up around this precious stuff. It was thought that spilling salt brought bad luck. Some people believed that the Devil caused the accident. To keep off the bad luck, a person must throw some of the salt over his left shoulder, hoping to hit the Devil in the eye and blind him. A bit of the superstition about salt's bad luck still exists among some people. It was immortalized by Leonardo da Vinci. In his famous painting, "The Last Supper," he showed a saltcellar tipped over by the arm of Judas.

22

One ancient belief held that birds could be caught by throwing salt on their tails (From an old engraving, New York Public Library)

The idea that salt could ward off evil was found in many ancient countries. Children in the Orient used to wear small bags of salt around their necks as a protection from harm. In many lands, salt was used in burial rites to protect the dead from evil. It was used in wedding ceremonies, to bring good fortune to the newlyweds. And it was scattered in new homes, to keep out evil spirits.

SALT IN GOVERNMENT AND SOCIAL LIFE

NATURALLY, RULERS wanted to control this powerful substance. Many laws were made to govern its manufacture and sale, and heavy taxes were imposed on it. In France the burdensome tax on salt and the punishment of tax evaders was one of the things that led to the French Revolution. In this century the unbearable tax on salt in India was one of the ills that led to the civil disobedience of the people under the famous Mahatma Gandhi.

Because of the slow and expensive methods of producing salt, and the heavy taxes put on it by rulers, salt was not an easy thing to come by. In fact, for many, many years only the rich could afford it on their tables. In Ethiopia a very rich man was called "he who eats salt."

The fortunate wealthy people showed their respect for the condiment by placing it in elaborate and beautiful saltcellars. Often these were made of gold or silver, inlaid with pearls and precious gems. In England the great saltcellar was placed halfway down the table. Nobles sat "above the salt." The common folks sat "below the salt."

The art of making saltcellars reached its peak in England in the sixteenth and seventeenth centuries, when the great "steeple" salt holders were produced. A little earlier, in Italy, such famous artists as Benvenuto Cellini and Leonardo da Vinci had directed their great genius to fashioning saltcellars that today may be found only in museums.

In several countries, salt was so valuable that it was used as money. In China only gold was more valuable than salt. In Tibet, and Ethiopia and other parts of Africa, salt cakes impressed with the ruler's insignia were used as money. In still other African communities a palm-leaf cylinder held five pounds of salt, the standard unit of exchange. Ten of these cylinders could purchase a wife. In Egypt, fifteen hundred years before Christ, the coins were salt cakes measuring approximately 8 by 4 by 2½ inches.

The Rospigliosi cup, made of gold, enamel, and pearls, by Benvenuto Cellini, 1500-1571 (The Metropolitan Museum of Art, Bequest of Benjamin Altman, 1913)

In the days of the Roman Empire, soldiers were paid partly in salt, or were given a certain amount of money with which to buy the salt they needed. This pay was called a *salarium*, from the Latin word meaning "of salt," and from it comes our word "salary." From this old Roman practice we also get the contemptuous phrase, "not worth his salt."

SALT BUILDS ROADS

WHEN PRIMITIVE MAN learned that he could trade lumps of salt for something else he wanted, the salt trade began and as time went on grew into an important business. Countries that had more salt than they needed found they could enrich their treasuries by sending salt to other lands. Those countries that had no supply had to send caravans into the salt centers to obtain what they needed. The roads to and from these salt centers became highways of travel. Some of the roads built for the salt trade are still in use today.

One of the oldest roads stretches across the Sahara from the oasis of Bilma in west Africa to the seaports on the coast. At Bilma a salt crust formed on the marshes. This was broken up, raked together, packed on camels' backs, carried to the ports, and from there shipped to Europe and Asia.

Camel caravans still make their slow way across the burning Sahara sands. Though a five-ton truck can carry as large a load as forty camels can, not much change has been made in the age-old transportation. Many of these desert creatures, each with 250 pounds of salt on its back, still amble across the desert.

In Italy the famous Via Salaria, the Salt Way, was used from immemorial time to carry salt from Ostia, near Rome, to the Sabine country in the northeast. Today the road is an automobile highway. In England the road from Chester to London began as a path over which salt from the Cheshire mines was brought to the port on the Thames, and from there was shipped across the channel to Gaul, now France.

In America, burro caravans carried salt from what is now Alamogordo, New Mexico, to the silver mines of Sonora, Mexico. U.S. Highway 70 now follows much of that old salt trail.

SALT AND CITIES

BECAUSE SALT CARAVANS traveled great distances they needed places to spend the night along the way. When they reached a port they might have to wait days or weeks for a ship to arrive. In those early times, ships had no regular schedules. Storms, errors in navigation, or mutiny might delay them. Therefore, along the caravan routes and at the ends of the trails, people gathered to build shelters and to supply food and other needs to the caravans. In time, such small groups of houses and shops grew into cities.

The fabulous city of Timbuktu in Africa grew from a cluster of huts built to shelter camel caravans. The American cities of Syracuse, New York; Lincoln, Nebraska; Saltsburg, Pennsylvania; Shawneetown, Illinois, and many others owe their beginnings to salt.

Lincoln, Nebraska, about a hundred years ago, when the salt wells nearby were an important part of the town's industry (Nebraska State Historical Society)

The quaint town of Hallstatt, in Austria, which grew up around the salt beds of the region

Workers in a present-day salt mine at Hallstatt, Austria, where modern machine methods have replaced the ancient ones

A world atlas lists scores of places whose names show that they began as salt cities. In England, towns with names ending in "wich," such as Norwich, Droitwich, and Greenwich, tell the story. "Wich" is the Saxon word for "a place where salt is dug." In Germany and Austria such towns may have either "salz" or "hall" in their names. You will remember that halite is the mineral term for salt.

The word for salt is similar in many languages. In German it is *salz*; in Russian, *sohl*; in French, *sel*; in Spanish, *sal*.

One of the Turks Islands is Salt Cay, whose main industry is gathering salt. Off the coast of Ireland are the Saltee Islands. An inlet of the Norwegian Sea is called Salt Fjord. A Scottish town has the name Saltcoats. In Ghana, in Africa, is a port called Saltpond.

One city showed its debt to salt in a strange way. In Lüneburg, Germany, near Hamburg, there used to be a glass case in front of the town hall. In this case were the moldering remains of a pig. The plaque on the case said: *Passerby, here you behold the mortal remains of a pig which acquired for itself imperishable glory through the discovery of the salt springs of Lüneburg.*

SALT IN COLONIAL AMERICA

THE FIRST RECORD of salt made by white men in America goes back to the settlers of Jamestown, Virginia. Needing salt, they boiled a sea herb and used the salty water to season their broth. "Other salt they knew not," says the record.

The ships that sailed to the New World often used salt as ballast. That is, the hold — the space beneath the deck — was filled with salt to weight the ship and make it more steady in the water. When they arrived at their destination, the captains sold this salt to the settlers, and filled the holds with fish, furs, and lumber for the return trip. Knowing how badly the salt was needed, the captains charged high prices for it.

The colonists needed a great deal of salt, not only for seasoning their food, but also for preserving the fish and furs they sent back to England. Their method of treating the fish was to place a layer of fish, cleaned and split, in square "beds" in the ship's hold. Over this layer was spread a thick covering of salt. Then more fish and more salt were added, one after the other, until the hold was filled.

After a time the settlers rebelled against paying the prices the captains asked for salt. They decided to make their own. Crude wooden vats were set up on the shore near Jamestown, and seawater was run into them. The settlers did not manage a very successful job, but they did get some salt from the evaporation of the seawater.

By 1630, saltworks had been established on the Eastern Shore of Chesapeake Bay. Thirteen years later, Virginia was making enough salt to be able to send some to her sister colony, Massachusetts. Massachusetts was having more difficulty in extracting salt from seawater, though its people were trying various methods.

At first, the governors of the colonies tried to control saltmaking, but as the need became more acute they offered prizes and bounties for successful saltworks. Queen Christina, in faraway Sweden, urged her colonists along the Delaware River, in New Sweden, to try to make salt for their own use.

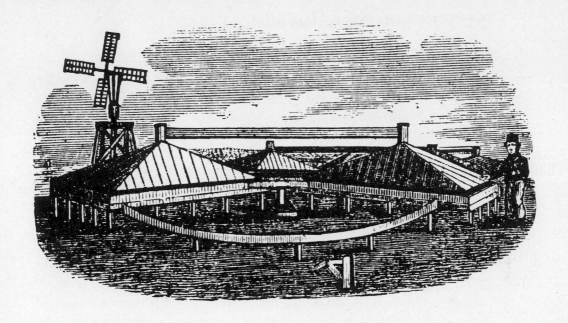

The early Cape Cod salteries had hinged roofs to protect the brine from rain-storms (From an old engraving, New York Public Library)

The very first patent issued in America, giving an inventor the exclusive right to make and sell his own product, was granted by the General Court of Massachusetts to Samuel Winslow in 1641, for the making of salt "by a meanes & way which hithero hath not been discovered." It was not a very successful way, and little salt was produced.

All along the coasts of Cape Cod, small salteries sprang up. Here, for the first time in America, the vats were covered with hinged roofs that could be drawn over to protect the brine from rainstorms. In other colonies, folks tried to make salt from seawater. One Dutch settler, Dirck de Wolff, had a plant on Coney Island. On the very spot where today a merry-go-round or a hot-dog stand may be operating he evaporated water in shallow wooden tubs.

SALT IN THE AMERICAN REVOLUTION

BY THE TIME of the American Revolution the colonies along the Atlantic coast were producing a fair part of the salt they needed. The rest was imported in British ships. Naturally, when the colonies went to war with England the supply from abroad was cut off and the home supply was in danger.

Fighting for control of a salt supply had become an old story long before this time. The colonists were well aware of this. They knew that not only would the British ships stop bringing in salt; they would also blockade the ports so that no other ships could come in. And the British soldiers would try to seize any saltworks possible. In December, 1775, the Continental Congress urged the governors of the colonies to encourage saltmaking. Later, the Congress offered a bounty of one-third of a dollar for every bushel of salt made or imported by the colonists.

As the war got under way, the British troops set out to capture any saltworks they could find. Early in the conflict they seized the salt springs near Lake Onondaga, in the central part of what is now New York State. And in 1777 they tried to capture the salt and other stores at Peekskill, New York.

Several small salteries had been set up in New Jersey at places where the Indians had long obtained salt. These were fair game for the British, who took and destroyed several of them. In 1782 a Tory refugee with "40 whites and 40 blacks" took Samuel Brown's works at Davenport, New Jersey. The Tories burned the works and set out southward, vowing to destroy every salt plant along the coast.

In Philadelphia there was a "salt party," similar to the Boston Tea Party. Three shiploads of salt sent to the British troops were seized, and the salt was dumped into the Delaware River. The whole affair was rather sad, because the people of Philadelphia really needed that salt. When hundreds of them died during the next winter, London newspapers triumphantly declared that the great death rate was due to lack of salt.

By the time independence had been won, the scarcity of salt had been so keenly felt that the new nation was determined never again to be caught without enough of it.

SALT IN THE WEST

BEFORE THOMAS JEFFERSON became President of the United States in 1801, Congress had passed an act requiring government surveyors to note carefully the location of every salt spring they found. Salt springs and wells were important, because the brine in them held much more salt than did seawater.

In 1804 President Jefferson sent out two men, Meriwether Lewis and William Clark, with an expedition to explore the Louisiana Purchase. Their journals describe the saltmaking methods of the Indian tribes they met, and their own efforts to obtain this needed mineral. Several of the party were set aside, as in Caesar's time, to be saltmakers. In January, 1805, the journals recorded that the men were getting from three quarts to a gallon of fine white salt a day. Clark wrote, "This was a great treat to myself and most of the party, having had none since the twentieth of last month."

At the end of the American Revolution the government had offered free land in the west to war veterans. Some of these veterans stopped at the salt springs near Onondaga Lake in New York. The Indians in the region boiled salt in open kettles over outdoor fires, and the settlers decided to follow this custom. At first, the Indians were reluctant to have the white men work at the springs. When Colonel Comfort Tyler won their confidence, however, they led him to the spring site, hidden in the woods.

A year later, in 1789, Nathaniel Loomis led a party into this area. He brought fifteen iron kettles, and in a short time was producing salt. By spring he had fifty bushels on hand, which he sold for one dollar a bushel. Other than that from seawater, this was the first salt in this country obtained for commercial purposes.

33

Saltmaking at Syracuse, New York, in 1857. Brine from nearby springs was evaporated in blocks of kettles (New York State Historical Association)

Other settlers arrived in the Onondaga area, and kettles were boiling day and night. Soon buildings were erected, brick ovens built, and great boilers constructed. Thousands of bushels of salt were sent east by wagon caravan, until 1825. In that year the Erie Canal was completed and, from then on, the salt could be shipped much more cheaply by canal barge. The Erie Canal is sometimes called "the ditch that salt built," because cheap transportation of salt was one of the reasons for its construction.

Workers on the canal used to sing:

> *We're loaded down with gin and salt.*
> *We're plumb chock full of rye.*
> *And the cap'n he looks down at us*
> *With a mean and wicked eye.*

In 1838 the railroad came to this New York region, and the saltmakers had still another means of sending their product to eastern cities. By this time there was a string of small salt towns around Lake Onondaga: Salina, South Salina, Syracuse, Liverpool, and Geddes. For many years

34

they produced the greatest part of the salt used in the United States. As time went on, Syracuse took over Salina and South Salina and became the leading salt city of the region.

All this time the boiling process had been used, with wood as fuel. Now the state government became worried at the way the forests were being cut down to keep the salt kettles boiling. Officials begged the manufacturers to try solar evaporation. The saltmakers knew that there was danger of summer rains spoiling the product. But they met the challenge by devising salt vats with hinged roofs, which could quickly be drawn over the ponds if a storm came up.

Today, common salt is not produced in great quantity in the Onondaga area, but salt brine is still used in the manufacture of several products important in the region's large chemical industry.

OTHER SALT FINDS

FARTHER SOUTH, westering emigrants crossed the Kanawha River in Virginia. Here again, some stopped to make settlements near salt springs where for centuries wild animals and Indians had satisfied their salt hunger.

In 1806, Daniel Boone lived in a cabin in the mountains north of the river. He had long made salt for himself, and now he helped the settlers establish saltworks. So the city of Charleston, later to become the capital of West Virginia, was born. By 1832, more than a million bushels of salt were produced here every year. Much of this was shipped up the Ohio River to Cincinnati, where it was used in curing pork. At that time, Cincinnati was the great meatpacking center of the country.

Due to a mixture of iron in it, Kanawha salt was of a reddish color. "That strong red Kanawha salt" was famous as a good preservative of meat. Today, however, as in the Onondaga area, the Kanawha brine is used chiefly in the manufacture of chemicals, not salt.

In Kentucky also, early emigrants started settlements near salt licks.

35

Long after towns had been established, salt-hungry buffalo still came to their old licks. One settler wrote of counting five hundred of the shaggy animals crowded around one spring.

Not only surveyors and settlers, but trappers and explorers also, were always on the lookout for salt sources to replenish their supply as they moved into unknown country. General William Ashley, who employed many mountain men, wrote in 1825 of the salt to be found around the Great Salt Lake. The famous pathmaker, John Charles Frémont, paused on the shore of the lake in 1842 while his men boiled water to get salt. To the southeast of this area, emigrant trains waited in the valley of the Cimarron River while men raked salt to carry with them.

SALT IN THE CIVIL WAR

WHEN THE CIVIL WAR broke out in 1861, Syracuse and the Kanawha Valley works were producing millions of bushels of salt each year. The works on Cape Cod, which had been carefully protected from the British during the War of 1812, were doing fairly well. In Nebraska, California, and Kansas, some salt was being produced. The Mormons, in Utah, could obtain from the Great Salt Lake all the salt they needed and more, though they did not start shipping it east until much later. With all this activity the North did not need to worry about salt.

The South, however, was in difficulty. It had no large saltworks and because of the North's blockading of its ports it could not import much salt. There were small salt ponds in Key West, Florida, but they were in the hands of Northern troops. When the Florida people in sympathy with the South tried to steal the salt, the ponds were drained and saltmaking was stopped.

The rich saltworks along the Kanawha River were fought for again and again. First the North, then the South, held them until 1863, when the South lost all hope of getting salt there.

There was another, less important, salt-producing region in Virginia,

An old engraving shows Saltville, Virginia, in 1857 (Virginia State Library)

at Saltville. Its saltworks had an unusual history. In 1755, Indians had kidnapped Mary Draper Ingles of Buffalo Lick, in southwest Virginia. As they traveled westward with their captive, the Indians paused at the Kanawha to make salt. Mary was forced to help them boil the brine. Later she escaped and managed to make her way home. She told her friends how the Indians made salt. "There are salt wells here, too," she said. "We can make salt as the Indians do."

This old engraving pictures a worker dipping salt from a brine kettle at Saltville, Virginia (Virginia State Library)

So from an unhappy experience came a new industry which changed the name of Buffalo Lick to Saltville. Here, at the time of the Civil War, some 200,000 bushels of salt a year were being made. The wells were the main salt supply for the entire South until they were lost to Union soldiers in 1864.

Near Arkadelphia, Arkansas, John Hemphill had started a saltworks in 1811. It didn't amount to much until the Confederate army took over. They drilled new wells, used discarded steamboat boilers, and put Negro slaves to work boiling brine day and night. But in the fall of 1863 General Frederick Steele's Union troops captured the works and stopped the flow of salt to the Confederate army.

When the Civil War was over, people remembered how important salt had been, and how expensive. Sometimes it had sold for as much as ten dollars a bushel. Sometimes it could not be bought at any price. Now folks set out to discover new and better sources of this vital mineral.

38

NEW DAYS, NEW WAYS

ALL THIS TIME, for some five thousand years that we know of, and probably for more besides, the methods of obtaining salt had not changed much, and scarcely any attempt had been made to improve the quality of the salt produced.

It was often bitter and of an ugly color. Much of it contained impurities that were actually harmful to the human body. But to us, nowadays, the ancient methods of cleansing it seem almost as bad as the impurities themselves. In Europe the whites of eggs were added to the boiling brine. They brought to the surface a scum of waste matter that could then be removed. In China, bean juice was used; in some countries the blood of black cattle was added; in the American colonies, melted tallow was poured into the brine — all for the same purpose: to clear the salt of impurities.

In addition, the old-time salt had an annoying way of forming into a hard lump, or caking, whenever the weather was a bit damp.

In 1748 William Brownrigg, an Englishman, wrote about saltmaking: "It is hard to understand how an art so simple and withal so necessary hath not been brought to any degree of perfection." Not until more than a hundred years after this time was any real change made in the old ways of obtaining salt.

In 1886, at Silver Springs, New York, a man named Joseph Duncan invented a device known as a vacuum-pan evaporator. A vacuum pan is a covered pan from which most of the air has been pumped. In such a pan, water will boil at a lower temperature than in an ordinary kettle.

People had long known that, when brine was boiled over a low fire, the salt was finer than when a hot fire was used. Now, when brine was boiled in a vacuum pan, the salt crystals were finer, whiter, and of more even size than ever before. This salt was called granulated salt, because the crystals resembled those of granulated sugar.

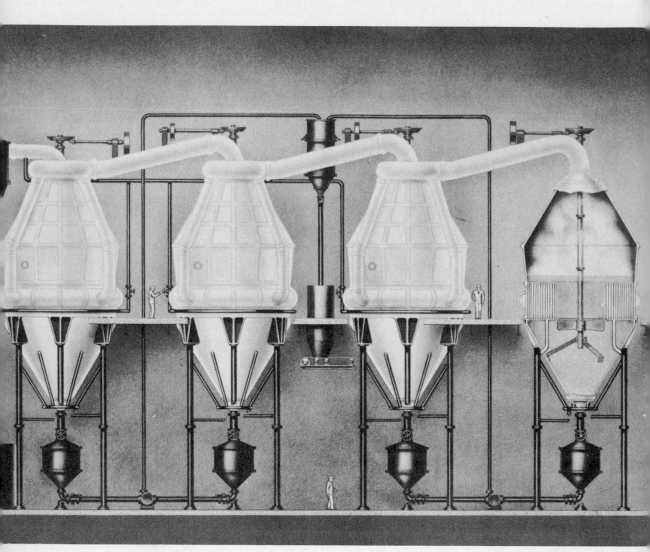

These four vacuum pans make a set through which brine is boiled to produce granulated salt. The human figures give an idea of their size (International Salt Company)

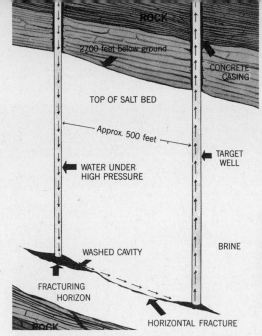

Brine can be obtained by running water over underground beds of salt. Sometimes two pipes are sunk side by side. Water is pumped down one pipe to the salt, then forced to the surface through the other (International Salt Company)

Oil-well drilling equipment is used to drive salt wells. When drilling is completed, this rig is moved away and all that remains on the surface is a "Christmas tree" of pipes, valves, and controls (International Salt Company)

The vacuum-pan evaporator was the first real breakthrough in the methods of producing salt. Other Americans set to work to make other improvements. Today the production of salt is a fast, efficient mechanical process.

Sometimes the brine that is needed is obtained from deep underground reservoirs of salt water, and sometimes it is obtained by running water over underground beds of rock salt. In this latter method, pipes are sunk anywhere from 750 to 7,000 feet to reach the beds. Sometimes two pipes are sunk side by side. Water is pumped into one pipe and forced down to the salt, dissolving it, and is then forced up to the surface through the second pipe. Sometimes, instead, a large pipe is sunk, and a smaller one is placed inside it. When a stream of fresh water is shot down between the two pipes it seeps through the salt bed. The salt slowly dissolves and brine forms, then is pumped up through the smaller, central pipe.

41

Air view of a salt plant at St. Clair, Michigan. Note the salt tanks in the left foreground (Fairchild Aerial Surveys)

Next, the brine is run into settling tanks, where the impurities are removed, not by bean juice or the blood of black cattle, but by chemicals that do a clean, efficient job.

The brine is then pumped into the vacuum pans, which are great covered tanks, three stories high. There are two or more tanks in a set. Steam is used to make the brine boil as it is pumped from tank to tank. As the brine boils, it is kept moving about until granules form. The mixture of salt granules and water is called slurry. The slurry is drawn off, and filtered to remove most of the moisture. Then the salt is thoroughly dried in huge revolving ovens.

Inside huge vacuum pans the circulating brine is boiled away by live steam (International Salt Company)

From all sides, parts come together, and round containers of salt emerge from automatic machines (International Salt Company)

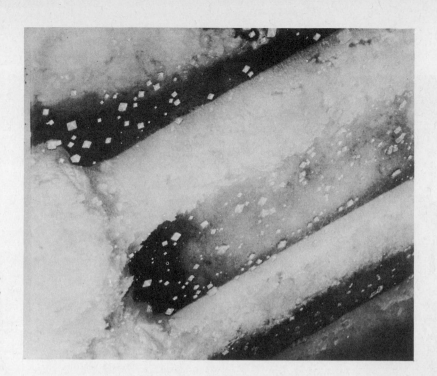

Crystals of "grainer," or flake, salt are formed on the surface of the heated brine (International Salt Company)

When it is dry it is run over a series of screens which separate the various grades of coarseness. The finest granules trickle through the first screen, and are sent through pipes to the packaging room. There the salt is automatically poured into boxes, for table use and for the making of butter, cheese, and bakery goods, or for canning and meat-packing. Coarser grades drop through coarser screens and are packaged and sold for freezing ice cream, for pickling, and for water-softening. The very coarsest granules may be used to melt the ice on winter roads, though sometimes crushed rock salt is used, instead.

In another modern boiling method, large, shallow open pans heated by steam are used. This process produces "grainer" salt. The salt forms on the surface of the heated brine and gradually sinks to the bottom of the pan, where it is scraped out by automatic rakes. This salt is in irregular-shaped crystals and is often thin and flaky. Salt of this kind is used on pretzels and some other food and dairy products. If it is extra coarse it may be pressed into salt blocks for animals.

Salt ponds at a saltworks in Utah. Dikes enclose about twenty thousand acres, where water from the Great Salt Lake is evaporated (Utah State Historical Society)

SOLAR EVAPORATION TODAY

THOUGH SOLAR EVAPORATION is still important in making salt in countries that do not have many machines or much electric power, it is not widely used in America today. The solar method is employed at the saltworks on the shore of the Great Salt Lake in Utah and at vast ponds along the coast of San Francisco Bay in California, however.

Let's take a look at the Utah plant. Here each spring, usually in May, water from the lake is pumped into square, shallow ponds near the shore. This water contains from 15 to 25 per cent of salt. It is left in the ponds until the sun's rays have evaporated much of the water, and the proportion of salt has increased until crystals are almost ready to form.

Now the brine is run into "garden" ponds, which are from 15 to 90 acres in size. They have a hard, foot-thick salt floor that over the years has been laid down on top of the clay soil of the area. In the garden ponds more evaporation takes place. The salt crystals form and sink to the bottom. The remaining water, called bittern because it has a bitter

46

A tractor disc plow breaks up the salt left by solar evaporation at a Utah saltworks (Utah State Historical Society)

taste, is pumped back into the lake. By the first of September a crop of salt from three to four inches thick has been left on the floor of the garden ponds. From four to five hundred tons of salt an acre can be harvested.

In harvesting, tractor-driven disc plows first break up the salt, then machines pick it up and carry it to stockpiles. There it lies until it is needed at the plant, where it is refined, dried, screened, and packaged, much as any other salt is.

Harvesting salt in the works on the shores of the Great Salt Lake in Utah. Electrically driven machines pick up the loosened salt and send it on a conveyor belt to a mountainous stockpile (Utah Tourist and Publicity Council)

MINING SALT

IN SOME PARTS of the United States, underground rock salt is mined, but the processes used are far different from the former hand-pick methods of Europe.

Some of the world's greatest salt deposits have been found under Detroit, Michigan, and on Jefferson and Avery islands, in Louisiana.

Mines at these places are worked entirely with great modern machines. From the earth's surface to the underground salt bed a shaft is dug. This provides ventilation, and space for an elevator that carries the workers up and down. For safety the shaft is usually lined with concrete.

In mining, an undercutting machine makes a slot in the face of the salt wall, down even with the floor. Another, vertical slot is made at each end of the section to be mined. Above the floor slot, holes are drilled, and an

Surface view of the Avery Island Mine and Refinery, Louisiana (International Salt Company)

The first step in preparing a salt wall for blasting is to undercut a channel ten feet deep and about six inches high at floor level (International Salt Company)

A drill rig makes holes in the mine face (International Salt Company)

Explosives in the mine face are wired for firing (International Salt Company)

The explosion in the mine face brings down hundreds of tons of salt (International Salt Company)

In this mine the crushed salt is carried upward on an automatic conveyor belt (International Salt Company)

explosive is set into the holes. When the men are at a safe distance, the explosive is set off by a switch. Hundreds of tons of salt, from mere dust to huge chunks weighing several hundred pounds, are blasted down.

A loading machine then gathers up the salt and empties it into cars that carry it to the dump station. There it is crushed and screened and hoisted to the surface of the earth, where it is placed in bins to await further crushing, purifying, and packaging.

A mine employee checks two banks of noisily vibrating salt screens (International Salt Company)

Crushers aboveground further break up the salt brought from the mine (International Salt Company)

Ceilings 100 feet high dwarf men and machines in the Avery Island Mine (International Salt Company)

In this way great rooms are excavated underground. Pillars of salt are left to support the ceilings. Because rock salt is twice as strong as brick, the workmen are safe from any chance of the mines' collapse. This way of mining is called the "room and pillar" method.

At one time great dinosaurs lived in the swampy marshes that covered much the land (Deseret News)

PLENTY OF SALT

WITH EVERY LIVING CREATURE needing salt, and with all its other uses too, is there any danger of the earth's supply becoming exhausted?

No. Almost since the earth was formed, hundreds of millions of years ago, salt has been washing out of the rocks. As long as they remain, more salt will constantly be added to our supply. At the same time, much of the "used" salt will not really disappear, but in various ways will be returned to the earth and to the lakes and seas.

The oceans of the world contain more salt than man can use within any forseeable time. On an average, one gallon of seawater holds approximately one-fourth of a pound of salt. Of course, all oceans are not equally salty. The Atlantic is more salty than the Pacific. The Red Sea and the Great Salt Lake are two of the saltiest bodies of water, with nearly two gallons of salt to every sixteen gallons of water. Polar seas are the least salty, because they are constantly being freshened by melting snow and ice.

If all the salt could be extracted from the Great Salt Lake in Utah, there would be enough to last the world for five hundred years

Many old lakes and seas have dried up and left their salt behind, as in these Texas salt flats (Texas Highway Department)

Many old lakes and seas have dried up and have left their salt behind. Such deposits are found in many parts of the world. Some have been used for thousands of years, and new ones are discovered from time to time.

The earth's surface today is far different from what it once was. During millions of years great changes have taken place. Geologists tell us that once much of what is now North America was covered by oceans or lakes. At some periods in the dim past great glaciers swept down over parts of the earth. At other times, forests and jungles grew where now there are mountains or plains or deserts.

The interior of the earth was not quiet. There were rumblings and upheavals. The crust wrinkled and cracked; mountains were thrust up. Waters of inland lakes drained into the oceans. Or perhaps an outlet was dammed off and the waters could not reach the sea. If this happened, the lake became saltier and saltier as it received material washed out of the rocks around it, and as the sun and wind evaporated its water. Salt lakes and inland seas were formed in this way.

The Dead Sea of Palestine was left behind by an arm of the Mediterranean, which has now vanished. The sea's waters are 25 per cent solid matter, which includes common salt, gypsum, potash, and other chemical substances.

The Great Salt Lake in Utah is about all that remains of prehistoric Lake Bonneville, which once covered much of Utah and spread into Nevada and Idaho. It has been estimated that Lake Bonneville took about fifty thousand years to shrink to the size of the present Great Salt Lake. The waters of this lake alone contain some six billion tons of salt — enough to last the world for many years.

LOST LAKES

SOMETIMES A LAKE did not dry up after an upheaval of the earth's crust. Instead, the whole lake slipped underground through a crack, or seeped down slowly through porous rocks, until it came to a hard bottom through which it could not go. There it lay, hidden deep in the earth — a dark, briny pool. Sometimes the pressure of the rocks around it forced the water up to the surface in wells or springs. Such reservoirs of salt brine are found under Michigan and in Asia and central Europe. The salt springs of Ohio, Kentucky, and New York show that such hidden pools lie below the surface in these regions.

In other places, water no longer remains. The salt crust that was left when the lake dried up has been buried deep beneath dirt and stone, and the weight of this overburden has pressed the salt into solid rock. Most

*At Redmond, in Utah, the covering of earth and rocks has been washed away,
leaving a mountain of rock salt exposed*

The lines of this wall in the Avery Island Mine in Louisiana show clearly how layers of salt formed, one on top of another, then were slowly pushed upward to make a dome (International Salt Company)

such deposits of rock salt are found deep under the earth's surface, but in some places the covering soil has been washed away, leaving a mountain of solid salt. Great rock-salt deposits are found in Poland, Austria, Russia, North Africa, and in several parts of North America.

In some regions the buried layers of salt were pressed and pushed so hard by the surrounding rocks and earth that they were driven upward into great plugs, or domes. Louisiana has more than a hundred such salt domes, laid down millions of years ago. Some of the domes are nearly five miles below the earth's surface, buried so deep that they might never have been found but with the help of instruments especially designed to discover the earth's hidden secrets. Some of these instruments are used chiefly for hunting oil. It was while searching for oil that men found the salt domes.

When we remember that salt in the earth is left by lost lakes and seas and that petroleum oil is often all that remains of the bodies of sea animals, we can see that it is natural for oil and salt to be found together. And so they are: pockets of oil are often located against the side of a salt dome.

But wherever salt is found — in a shrinking lake, a lake lost under the earth's surface, a layer of rock, or a dome — there at some time, past or present, a lake or sea has covered the land.

59

SALT IN INDUSTRY AND DAILY LIFE

MOST OF THE SALT produced today is not used as common salt. Nearly three-fourths of it is broken down into sodium and chlorine and is used in industry.

The world produces some 95 million tons of salt a year. The United States leads all other countries, with more than 25 million tons — more than one-fourth of the total world production. Seven states yield the largest part of this salt: Louisiana, Texas, Michigan, New York, Ohio, California, and Kansas.

Germany, the United Kingdom, Italy, France, and India are also big salt producers. It is uncertain how much salt China is producing now, but in 1950 that country ranked fourth among the nations in this industry.

The millions of tons of salt produced each year in the United States average about 280 pounds for every man, woman, and child in the country. Of this amount, only seventy pounds are used by each person as common salt. It is estimated that every person consumes some six pounds of salt a year at meals; six pounds in processed foods; and fifty-eight pounds in other ways. The remainder of each person's allotment is found in his clothing, medicines, manufactured goods, and in a great variety of other things in the modern world around him. Salt is indeed important.

DO YOU KNOW

— that the purity of salt increases with the depth of the salt deposit?

— that Saltair, in Utah, was once a famous resort? This Moorish-style wooden pavilion, built on pilings driven into the Great Salt Lake, was built in 1890, but has been abandoned in recent years.

— that relics found in California indicate that men were living there and eating salt five thousand years ago?

— that Sequoya, the inventor of the Cherokee alphabet, operated a small saltworks in Arkansas?

Saltair, Great Salt Lake, in the days when it was a favorite bathing resort (Deseret News)

— that some streets in modern Syracuse, New York, carry names that come from the time when this was the Salt City? The main street is Salina (from the Latin word for "saltworks"); Cooper Street is where coopers, or barrelmakers, formerly made the salt barrels; Division Street marks the boundary between fighting crews of salt workers.

— that Indian pictographs in Arizona indicate the routes taken by Pueblo Indians to the salt caves in the Grand Canyon?

— that Nevada has salt wells and a salt desert with salt more than 98 per cent pure, yet scarcely any salt is produced in that state?

— that Salt Lake City once had a Salt Palace made of blocks covered with rock salt? When illuminated by hundreds of electric lights, it glistened like a fairy palace.

— that in olden times in China a man who stole a pound of salt was executed for the crime?

— that Pueblo Indians of Isleta, New Mexico, formerly presented an image of Salt Woman at their harvest festival? It was believed that anyone who thought bad things in her presence would turn into an animal when he died.

— that some people believe that bad luck will come if salt is not the first thing placed on the table?

— that the Finnish people have a legend that when Ukko, the Thunder God, first struck fire, some sparks fell into the ocean and turned to salt?

WORDS SALTMAKERS USE

BITTERN — The bitter liquid remaining after salt crystals form.

BRINE — Water heavy with salt.

BRINE OVENS — Brick or clay fireplaces in which kettles are placed for boiling brine.

CORN — Salt crystals. To "corn" means to form crystals.

FALL — The dropping of salt crystals to the bottom of the pan or pond.

HALITE — Rock salt.

SALIMETER — A device for measuring the amount of salt in brine.

SALINE — A place where salt marshes or springs are found.

SALTER — A salt worker (British).

SALTERIES — Saltworks.

SALT GARDEN — A pond in which salt crystallizes.

SALT GROUND — A field where salt is evaporated.

SALT HOUSE — A building in which salt is made.

SALT PAN — A kettle in which brine is boiled.

SLURRY — A mixture of salt crystals and brine.

SWEET SALT — Common salt.

INDEX

Africa, 24, 26, 27
Agricola, 17
Air, salt in, 16
American Revolution, 32
Animals
  importance of salt to, 4, 5-6, 8-9
Antelope Island, 10
Arizona, 61
Arkadelphia, Arkansas, 38
Arkansas, 38, 60
Ashley, General William, 36
Atlantic Ocean, 55
Avery Island, Louisiana, 48, 59
Aztecs, 22

Bad Ischl, 21
Bible, 22
Big Bone Lick, Kentucky, 6
Bilma, Africa, 26
Bird refuges, 9
Birds, salt-encrusted, 16
Bittern, 46-47, 62
Blood, human
  salt in, 3-4
Body, human
  importance of salt to, 3-4, 12
  makeup of, 3
  salt in, 3, 4, 5
Boilers, 18, 34
Boiling, 13, 16, 17, 18, 19, 30, 33, 35, 36, 38,
  39
Boone, Daniel, 35
Brine, 31, 35, 41, 42, 45, 46, 57, 62
  clearing of, 39, 42
Brine ovens, 62
British Guiana, 16
Brownrigg, William, 39
Buffalo Lick, 37, 38

Caesar, 19
California, 36, 46, 60
California Indians, 20
Camels, 26
Cape Cod, 31, 36
Caravans, salt, 26, 27, 34
Cellini, Benvenuto, 24, 25
Cells, body, 3

Charleston, West Virginia, 35
China, 24, 39, 60, 62
Chlorine, 14, 60
Cimarron River, 36
Civil War, 36-38
Clark, William, 33
Cobalt, 8
Colonies, American, 30-32, 39
Coney Island, 31
Corn, 62
Crystals, salt, 2, 12, 39, 45, 46
Cyclic salt, 16

Dead Sea, 20, 57
Deserts, 10, 61
Detroit, Michigan, 20, 21, 48
Duncan, Joseph, 39

Earth, surface of, 56-57
Egypt, 20, 24
Element, 14
Embalming, 13
England, 16, 19, 24
Erie Canal, 34
Evaporation, 13, 14, 16-19, 30, 31
Evaporation, solar, 17-18, 35, 46-47
Evaporator, vacuum-pan, 39, 41, 42

Fall, 62
Farm stock, 6, 8
Fish, preservation of, 13, 30
Food, preservation of, 35
Foods, salt in, 3, 4
France, 18, 60
Frémont, John Charles, 36
French Lick, Indiana, 6
Furs, preservation of, 30

Gandhi, Mahatma, 24
Garden ponds, 46, 47
Geddes, New York, 34
Germany, 60
Grainer salt, 45
Grand Canyon, 61
Great Salt Lake, 9, 10, 12, 16, 36, 46, 55, 57,
  60, 61
  amount of salt in, 57

Halite, 14, 29, 62
"Hall," 29
Hemphill, John, 38
Hopi, 22

India, 16, 24, 60
Ingles, Mary Draper, 37
Iodine, 8
Iron, 8
Isleta, New Mexico, 62
Italy, 17, 60

Jamestown, Virginia, 30
Jefferson, Thomas, 33
Jefferson Island, Louisiana, 48

Kanawha River, 35, 36, 37
Kanawha salt, 35
Kansas, 36, 60
Key West, Florida, 7, 36

Lake Bonneville, 57
Lake Onondaga, 32, 33, 34, 35
"Last Supper, the," 22
Lewis, Meriwether, 33
Licks, 5-6, 12, 35, 36
Lincoln, Nebraska, 27
Liverpool, New York, 34
Loomis, Nathaniel, 33
Louisiana, 48, 59, 60
Lüneberg, Germany, 29

Marshlands, salt, 9
Massachusetts, 30, 31
Michigan, 57, 60
Mineral, 14
Mineral additives, 8
Minerals, body, 8
Mining, 20, 21, 48-53
Money, salt as, 24
Myths, 14, 15

Navahos, 22
Nevada, 10, 61
New Sweden, 30
New York, 32, 33, 57, 60, 61

Oceans, 14, 55
   proportion of salt in, 55
Ohio, 57, 60

Oil, 59
Ovens, 18, 34, 42

Pacific Ocean, 55
Packaging, 45
Patent, first in America, 31
Pet licks, 9
Petroleum, 59
Philadelphia, 32
Pictographs, Indian, 61
Plants
   and salt, 10
Plasma, 3
Poland, 20
Portugal, 18
Production, salt, 13, 16-19, 30, 31, 33-35, 36,
   37, 38, 39-47
Pueblo Indians, 61, 62

Red Sea, 55
Religious ceremonies, salt in, 22
Rock salt, 6, 20, 41, 45, 48, 53, 57, 59
Room and pillar method, 53
Rospigliosi cup, 25

Sahara, 20, 26
Sal, 29
Salarium, 25
Salary, 25
Salimeter, 62
Salina, New York, 34, 35
Saline, 62
Salt
   amount produced per year, 60
   and cities, 27-28
   harvesting of, 47
   in history, 12-13, 16-21, 24-38
   importance of, 3-6, 8
   in industry, 60
   myths about, 14, 15
   as a preservative, 1, 13, 22, 30, 35
   production of, 13, 16-19, 30, 31, 33-35, 36,
      37, 38, 39-47
   religious importance of, 22
   and roads, 26
   uses of, 1-3, 13, 30, 35, 45, 60
   world production of, 60
Salt blocks, 6, 8-9, 45
Salt Cay, 29
Salt domes, 59

Salt Fjord, 29
Salt flats, 10, 56
Salt-free diet, 5
Salt garden, 62
Salt goddess, 22
Salt, granulated, 39
Salt ground, 62
Salt hay, 10
Salt house, 62
Salt hunger, 4
Salt Lake City, 61
Salt lakes, 14, 57
Salt licks, 5-6, 12, 35, 36
Salt Man, 22
Salt mines, 20, 21, 29, 48-53
Salt Palace, 61
Salt pan, 62
"Salt party," 32
Salt plants, 19
Salt plugs, 59
Salt ponds, 17, 18, 36, 46
Salt-producing countries, 60
Salt-producing states, 60
Salt springs, 2, 32, 33, 35, 57
Salt supply, earth's, 55
Salt tablets, 1, 4
Salt water, 2, 10, 13, 14, 15, 16-20, 30, 41
Salt wells, 18, 33, 37, 38, 57, 61
Salt Woman, 22, 62
Saltair, 60, 61
Saltcellars, 24
Saltcoats, 29
Saltee Islands, 29
Salter, 62
Salteries, 62
Saltmaking, 13, 16-19, 30-31, 33-35, 36, 37, 38,
    39-47
Saltpond, Ghana, 29
Saltsburg, Pennsylvania, 27
Saltville, Virginia, 38
Saltworks, Chinese, 18
"Salz," 29
Salzburg, Austria, 21

Sambhar Lake, 16
Screening, 45
Sculpture, salt, 20, 21
Seas, inland, 57
Seawater, 13, 20, 22, 30, 31
    boiling of, 13, 17, 18, 19
    evaporation of, 13, 16-19
Seaweeds, 19
Sel, 29
Sequoya, 60
Shawneetown, Illinois, 27
Slurry, 42, 62
Sodium, 2, 14, 60
Sodium chloride, 14
Sohl, 29
South Salina, 34, 35
Sulphur, 8
Superstitions, 22, 23, 62
Sweet salt, 62
Syracuse, New York, 27, 34, 35, 61

Taxes, salt, 24
Texas, 60
Thailand, 19
Tibet, 24
Timbuktu, 27
Trade, salt, 13, 26
Tyler, Colonel Comfort, 33

Ukko, 62
Underground lakes, 57
United Kingdom, 60
U. S. Highway 70, 26
Utah, 9, 10, 16, 46, 55, 57, 60, 61

Vats, 30, 31, 35
Vinci, Leonardo da, 22, 24
Virginia, 30, 35, 36-38

"Wich," 29
Wieliczka, 20
Winslow, Samuel, 31
Wolff, Dirck de, 31